PODCAST AUTHORIZED

PODCAST AUTHORIZED

How to Turn Your Podcast into a Book
to Build Your Business

JENN FOSTER
MELANIE JOHNSON
STEVE GORDON

Podcast Authorized: How to Turn Your Podcast into a Book to Build Your Business

Copyright © 2020 Elite Online Publishing

All rights reserved. No part of this publication may be reproduced, distributed, or transmitted in any form or by any means, including photocopying, recording, or other electronic or mechanical methods, without the prior written permission of the publisher, except in the case of brief quotations embodied in critical reviews and certain other noncommercial uses permitted by copyright law.

Publisher:
Elite Online Publishing
63 East 11400 South Suite #230
Sandy, UT 84070
www.EliteOnlinePublishing.com

Second Edition: October 2020

Cover Design by Jenn Foster

Printed in the United States of America

ISBN: 978-1513660493

Table of Contents

INTRODUCTION	3
CHASING CLIENTS IS OBSOLETE	3
THE POWER OF A PODCAST AND A BOOK TOGETHER	9
FOUR BENEFITS OF A PODCAST	12
#1 CREATING STRATEGIC RELATIONSHIPS	14
#2 THE FOREVER FOLLOW-UP	16
#3 DEMONSTRATE YOUR EXPERTISE	18
#4 DEVELOP INTELLECTUAL PROPERTY	19
CREATING VALUE AND PURPOSE	21
THREE WAYS TO ADD VALUE	25
GIVE YOUR BOOK AWAY	28
CALL TO ACTION	33
POWER OF A BOOK	34
WRITING THE BOOK THAT WRITES ITSELF	37
EASY STEPS TO WRITING A BOOK!	37
WHY PUBLISH A BOOK — NOW!	39
REPURPOSE YOUR CONTENT	48
THE PERFECT EXAMPLE	49
A FEW TIPS ON YOUR BOOK CONTENT	51
BECOME AN EXPERT — INTERVIEW EXPERTS	52
SOMEONE INTERVIEWS YOU!	54
USE A.I.	55
INTERVIEW YOURSELF ON CAMERA	56

PROS AND CONS	56
THE 10X3X3 WRITING FORMULA	57
YOU'RE NOT RECREATING THE WHEEL	59

PUBLISH YOUR BOOK! 61

A WINNING TITLE	62
BOOK TITLE SAMPLES	62
BOOK COVER	65
BOOK MARKETING AND PROMOTIONS	67

BOOK AND PODCAST BEST PRACTICES 71

HOW TO RECORD A PODCAST	71
HOW TO PUBLISH A BOOK	73
WHAT FORMAT WILL YOUR BOOK BE?	74
BESTSELLER CAMPAIGN	77

HOW TO MAKE MONEY WITH A BOOK 79

TEN WAYS TO MAKE MONEY FROM YOUR BOOK TODAY	80
#1 WEB PAGE GIVEAWAY	80
#2 PRE-FRAME A MEETING	82
#3 FOOT IN THE DOOR: GETTING PAST THE GATEKEEPER	83
#4 MEETING WITH A VIP OR CELEBRITY	85
#5 GET SPEAKING GIGS	86
#6 TRADE SHOWS & EVENTS	87
#7 CALL TO ACTION	89
#8 FREE GIVEAWAYS	90
#9 JOINT VENTURES	91
#10 MEDIA ATTENTION AND PRESS RELEASES	93
BONUS: CHARGE MORE MONEY	95

PRODUCING A PODCAST AND PUBLISHING A BOOK 97

ESTABLISHING YOUR CREDIBILITY WITH A BOOK	98
ESTABLISHING YOUR CREDIBILITY WITH A PODCAST	100

ABOUT THE AUTHORS — 109

JENN FOSTER	109
MELANIE CHURELLA JOHNSON	113
STEVE GORDON	117
ACKNOWLEDGMENTS	119

FREE BONUS

From Jenn Foster and Melanie Johnson:
Easily write your book using our **Mindset Tool Kit.**

Visit EliteOnlinePublishing.com/bonus

Mindset Toolkit

From Steve Gordon:

Download my latest book *free* at

UnstoppableCEO.net/exponentialnetwork

The Exponential Network Strategy the book

INTRODUCTION
Chasing Clients is Obsolete

What if a previous prospect wanted to hang out with you for an hour, whereas before you couldn't even get your foot in the door?

What would it be worth to you if your favorite prospective client kept all your expertise on their nightstand or on their desktop?

Podcasting and books are like standing in a lake of kerosene, striking matches. The two work so well together that there should be a warning label.

By design, the traditional Funnel Stage Marketing is cumbersome and unforgiving. The Sales Funnel once offered a valuable path to success — as long as you kept shoveling new prospects into the top of the funnel, you're bound to see profits spit out of the bottom.

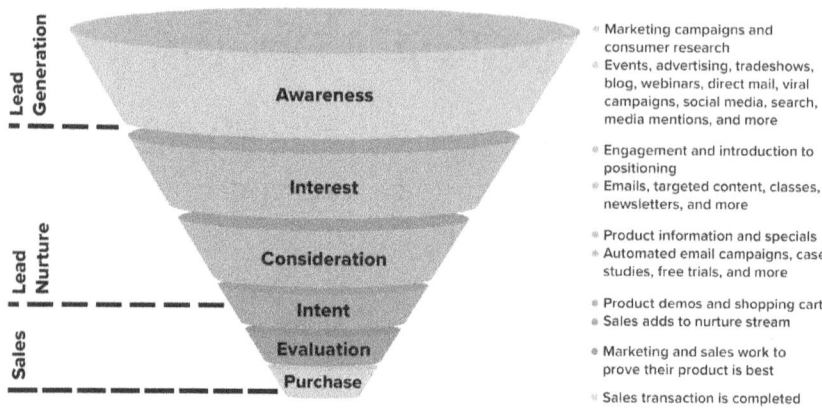

(Image source: How the Marketing Funnel Works from Top to Bottom, by Rebecca Lee White)

However, this also guarantees you will lose more business than you attract, because at every level, the prospect can disqualify themselves from your process, no matter how much time and money you have funneled into their procession. As your prospect steps through your funnel, he is asked, "are you aware," "are you interested," "would you consider," exhausting both the assessor and the assessed. Instead of beating the prospected with unexciting, unending, pre-qualifying questions, we would prefer generating the prospect's interest and compelling the consideration of the topic's product or service. If you're waiting for the person to grow inner excitement, then you will be waiting a very long time. During that time, you will be forced to pour more prospective leads into the top of your funnel to keep up with the slippage at every crack and crevice, only to have them disqualify themselves since they cannot self-generate enough excitement to stay in your funnel.

Today's modern marketer must understand the unprecedented changes in consumer behavior over a brief period. Companies must understand the shift in the balance of power between brands and learn how to build processes that guide prospects through their journey from purchase to loyalty. It's not about leads. It's about time and recourses to turn your prospects into brand ambassadors.

Podcasting doesn't reduce the number of stages in the sales process, but it switches never-ending questionable surveys for positive pressure, applied when needed. Instead of asking unending pre-qualifying questions, you are offering opinions to the listener on why they should be interested and why they should consider the offering.

In the early days of TV and Radio, audiences found most programming boring. The jokes fell flat until the American sound engineer Charles "Charley" Douglass invented the laugh track to cue the audience to laugh in the right places. This spurred on more laughter, more interest, until the laugh track became a standard in mainstream television in the U.S., dominating most prime-time sitcoms from the late 1950s to the late 1970s. The open mic podcast has replaced the laugh track for your sales funnel marketing, teaching your listeners what is essential, what is exciting, and what should be considered attractive. No longer leaving comprehension to chance, the podcast walks the listener to a better understanding of why they are interested and why they are spending time with you instead of your competitor.

Multiply your effectiveness ten-fold when you add a book to your podcasting. Motivated by face-to-face, trust-building podcasts, your readers will get to know you on an intimate level through your writing. Your customers quickly learn about you and your brand, streamlining the purchase process and forming loyalty within a matter of days instead of weeks or months. This is with little to no slippage, since it produces the *interested* instead of polling for results; therefore generating new business.

In my book journey, I took practical steps to make every effort a success, every step was a determined thoughtful move forward, and every learning experience only experienced once. I've earned the skills and knowledge, as well as compiled best and worst examples, to help you avoid mistakes while capitalizing on the triumphs. It can help you understand how it applies to every business. Using a book paired with a podcast generates a virtually endless supply of leads for your business, month after month. We will break down those steps necessary to create an infinite stream of interested clients, as well as how and why most authors fail.

After seeing hundreds of authors produce good books only to see their frustration when the book fails to provide the wanted and/or needed, expected results. I met Melanie and Jenn of Elite Online Publishing on a podcast interview and together we created inspiring guidelines, which allows anyone to produce their desired results *every* time. We will show you where the potholes are on this journey, so you can avoid them. We will give tips on how to finish your book quickly by teaching you how some books actually *can* write themselves.

We also will digest the book-authoring process, starting with how a book topic is selected, not by magic or a serendipitous toss of the dice, but rather clearly defining parameters to topic a book that will spur fascination for your readers and your prospects. Melanie also will delve into the best approaches to the writing process, so that even if you're not a natural writer, you'll be able to effortlessly produce a successful book regarding just about any topic your heart desires. We have included an entire chapter on marketing strategies to capitalize on your efforts to turn a profit at every step in the process. This collaboration has been on the workbench for a couple of months, and I think it's been one of the most significant experiences in my professional career. This book was written for us by recording our webinar and transcribing it. This has been one of the easiest books I've ever written.

If you are a business owner wanting to create a never-ending stream of new clients and contacts for every aspect of your business, then this book will be exciting for you. If you are interested in writing a book that seems to write itself, then this book will be motivating to you. If deep into your heart's desire is to write the next great American novel and become a modern-day F. Scott Fitzgerald, then sadly, you are probably not in the right place. However, you might want to check out the marketing strategies just in case you want to sell your book once you are published.

For authors who have written a book and want to get much better results, and entrepreneurs who maybe have a book idea, but not quite sure where to start, you're going to walk away with your arms full.

— Steve Gordon

1

THE POWER OF A PODCAST AND A BOOK TOGETHER

— Steve Gordon

The idea of writing a book can seem daunting, but we're here to tell you how to effortlessly create your own book and use it to attract high-ticket clients. This book is filled with proven ideas and techniques that currently are working for us, as well as our clients. You will learn how simple it is to repurpose your current content into a book or a podcast. We'll be using a lot of real-life examples as we detail marketing techniques and tools to write your own book and create your own podcast.

I'm Steve Gordon, a bestselling author of four books and the host of *Unstoppable CEO* Podcast. My first book completely transformed my business. *Podcast Prospecting* was written in 2017. I started using it with my podcast and it became clear to me that having a book is the best lead generator. In fact, of all the marketing tools I've tried, there's nothing that quite compares to a book. Webinars, email lists, and social media platforms all have their place, but books enhance each and every one of these areas, creating high quality leads.

Podcast Prospecting the book

What is the perceived value of a book? When we look at a book that might cost only 10 dollars, the value we get out of that book often can be in the millions of dollars. Who hasn't read a book that has changed their life or business in a meaningful way? A book can create tremendous results for your business and clients. Consider this: if you see a book that speaks to a problem you're seeking to solve, isn't that something you'll check out and quickly purchase, because it's an inexpensive and high-value method to get needed information. That's exactly why books work so well. They work better than articles, blogs, brochures, or flyers. When you package your knowledge into a book, it immediately has a higher perceived value and will generate the right kind of leads, customers, and media attention.

Steve Gordon, Founder, The Unstoppable CEO™

You're probably wondering at this point why there is such an emphasis on podcasts and books. Well, the answer is simple. Books and podcasts, when used together, are perfectly aligned to create a solid marketing plan. Time and time again we saw the same amazing results. Lead after lead came in through our landing page. *The reason?* Inside the first few pages of my book I included a Call to Action (CTA)! A CTA leads the prospect to a landing page for a free offer. The free offer needs to be compelling and give your prospective client something of value. Ask yourself, what does your client want? What value are they seeking? It should come as no surprise that we are a big proponent of books in and of themselves, but when you combine your podcast and book together, the results are endless.

Four Benefits of a Podcast

Podcasts are a simple way to create relationships and the easiest way to create a plethora of marketing content. Back in 2012, I wrote an email every weekday. At 5 a.m., I'd send out an email. The writing was a lot of work, as well as a lot of time and energy for someone who's not a natural writer. How do podcasts solve this problem? Now all I'm required to do is show up to my podcast interview. I meet with interesting people and build great relationships that lead to other collaborative opportunities, as well as new business. After the interview, my marketing team takes our creative ideas, spoken during podcasts, and turns them into emails, social media posts, and other marketing content. Doesn't this sound like something you'd like to do to make your life easier? A perfect example of this process is how *this* book got written. I was a guest on Jenn Foster and Melanie Johnson's podcast, *Elite Expert Insider*. Before and after the recorded interview, we built a relationship. This conversation then turned into a joint webinar regarding how books and podcasts complement one another. That webinar became this book.

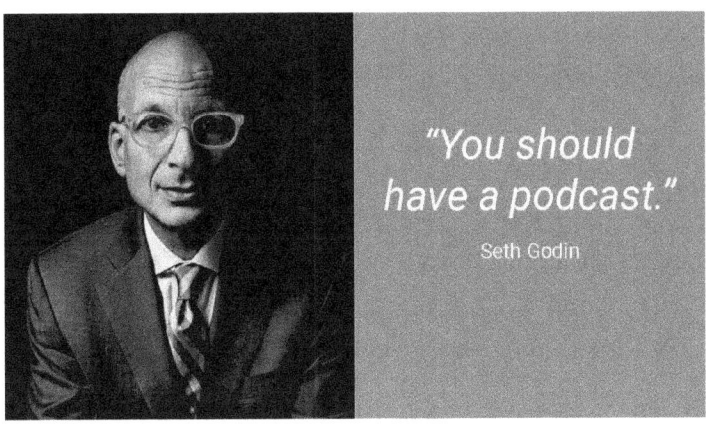

"You should have a podcast." Seth Godin

Seth Godin, former Vice President of Yahoo's direct marketing and author of 18 books, says you should have a podcast, and because he is Seth Godin, we're inclined to agree with him. He also said that "Podcasting is the new blogging." There really is no easier medium right now for you to get your message out.

The biggest problem that most businesses face is no one knows who you are. You are obscure, you need to get your name out there. You are the best-kept secret in your market. The great advantage of a podcast is through the sole power of your voice. It allows you to have a natural conversation, speak directly into the microphone, while getting your message out there. A podcast is better than blogging. Blogging is a form of creating content. You know, the kind where you go into your office or the writing cave, and type away. It's something done in solitary, but that's not the way business works. The best results in business come from relationships. Podcasting allows you to not only create content, but develop relationships and collaborate with other businesses. It allows you to multiply your results instantly. You are not going to post an article and hope someone sees it. With a podcast, you already have created a built-in motivation for at least one other person and they can share it with everyone they know — and it builds from there!

Akimbo, a podcast from Seth Godin

#1 Creating Strategic Relationships

Gary Vaynerchuk, a Belarusian-American entrepreneur, *New York Times* bestselling author, speaker, Internet personality, and a cofounder of Resy and Empathy Wines, stated the other day on LinkedIn, that "starting a niche podcast is one of the most incredible opportunities for anyone in B2B." Podcasting works for Adam King, the Captain of

Think Like a Fish, and host of *The Client Catching Podcast*. Adam's passion is helping service businesses, advisors, and experts to build their own "Client Catching Ecosystem" that removes you from up to 90% of your marketing and sales process, instantly boosts your authority, while at the same time increases the quality of leads, appointments, and clients that you attract and catch — All without spending a penny on advertising or adding more hours to your week!

Gary Vaynerchuk

Why are we such big proponents of podcasts? It allows you the freedom to do a lot of different things, such as creating strategic partnerships and relationships. This is the most important reason to have a podcast. We would record podcasts even if nobody listened. Sounds crazy, right? It's not. While we are beyond thankful for our listeners, the majority of the value in any podcast comes from the relationships you build with your invited guests. If you do this thoughtfully, you'll be able to create these relationships with other businesses with which you would never have connected via any other medium. A podcast gives you a place where they can come and promote themselves, they are going to show up. Not only that, but they are going to be excited about it! It allows you to be the buyer — you always want to be the buyer. You want to be the one that is buying rather than the one that's trying to sell someone or convince them to join you. When you invite someone as a guest to your podcast, you are buying them. You are giving THEM the opportunity to shine. This puts you in a powerful position. As you start these relationships you will find it's extremely effective.

Melanie and Jenn interviewed a man on their podcast just two weeks ago. He was launching his digital training course and looking for strategic partners. Jenn and Melanie jumped on board and helped sell his course through an affiliate link. In return, he interviewed them on his podcast where they gave away a book for free. Here was the CTA: Text your name and email to 58885 with the keyword *elite* to receive the book *How to Write Your Story of Accomplishment and Success*. When the podcast and digital training course were released, Melanie and Jenn received 75 leads in the first four days. This is the power of a strategic partnership.

#2 The Forever Follow-up

Businesses should investigate and consider podcasting as another channel for marketing, sales, service, communications, and branding, because the medium is in serious growth mode right now: (source: https://www.business2community.com/)

Statistics:
- One in three Americans listen to podcasts monthly
- One in four Americans listen to podcasts weekly
- Podcast listeners are affluent – more likely to make more than $75,000 per year
- More than half of listeners are more likely to consider buying an advertised product

A podcast allows you to create the forever follow-up. One of the biggest challenges we see in businesses at the start of our relationship is that they have many leads they have generated over the years, but they haven't pursued them. With just a small amount of work every month, you create that follow-up. Your leads will be going onto their podcast list, receiving an email every time a new episode is posted. It's an instant follow-up, one that is relevant to them. It's not just a sales pitch. You connect instantly with your leads. It also provides information for your social media content. A simple 30-minute interview will provide five to 10 quotes, and those quotes can become social media content. You also can pull images from it and can create a wide array of content.

You can tag the person interviewed on your podcast, connecting another world of listeners. The content then begins a snowball effect.

Take advantage of previous podcast episodes and re-post it on social media. Tag the person you interviewed and start the engagement in your comments. The interviewee will see this and encourage them to get engaged. Melanie and Jenn implemented this and out of the blue the interviewee called them to suggest a new client who was ready to write a book. One post on social media turned into an instant client.

#3 Demonstrate Your Expertise

Having a podcast gives you the opportunity to demonstrate your expertise in real-time. This is a very powerful tool, and yes, if you're showing up every week or every other week and you're doing an interview or having a conversation, you're establishing your credibility. When you're doing an interview, you are having a conversation — you are not grilling the person on the other end, like you might imagine an interview to be. While you are discussing your experience, the other person shares their expertise in their area. You'll be able to comment and contribute. It's a natural flow. Over time, your listeners hear that natural flow of conversation. They hear the real depth of expertise on the topic. The listeners also develop a relationship with you.

One of my listeners reached out to say that he had been listening to my podcast for hours as he traveled on a business trip. He didn't have to be convinced or receive a fancy sales pitch — he was ready to become my client. That is the power of a podcast, it lets you build relationships on a scale you just can't do otherwise.

#4 Develop Intellectual Property

The last big benefit of a podcast is you get to develop your intellectual property. As you talk through your message, your message gets refined, very quickly. You can take it even one step further and organize your episodes. For example, each episode could be a different chapter in a book. You could then hand that off to a ghostwriter or editor — it's a very easy way to create content and develop your intellectual property. This very book was created from a webinar we turned into a podcast. You get a lot of bang for a very small investment. We're talking maybe two to four hours a month of total time invested. For most, it takes that much time to write one decent article, sometimes more. When you have a podcast the results are limitless.

PODCAST AUTHORIZED

2

CREATING VALUE AND PURPOSE

— Steve Gordon

Back in 2012, I started my very first podcast called *The Small Business Marketing Show*. I ran it weekly for a year and interviewed 52 entrepreneurs over the course of 12 months. At that time, my entire database: prospects, partners, and clients was less than 500. I didn't have the contacts I do now, but I interviewed 52 people. The reason the podcast came to an end was because it worked. I even got a new business out of it!

How to turn your guests into a book promotion army

The reason I came back to the world of podcasting was to write a book and decided to get serious about it in 2014. I wrote every day and it took a full 365 days to complete the book. It was a lot of manual labor, but it doesn't have to be! The good news is you can write a book in a few days.

When you have a podcast, you can reach out to those with whom you built relationships and say, "I've got this book coming out, would you be willing to share it with people in your network or audience?" You also can reach out to those who have listened to your podcast via newsletter and social media to let them know that you now have a published book that they can read. It's a great way to generate leads! Those leads and those readers then refer your book and podcast to others. With these referrals, one can transform their business overnight and experience consistent steady growth. This lead generation will continue for years to come — that's the power of publishing a book! Not only having a book *published*, but the relationships built behind it will help you promote it and have success. What holds many back is they get the book published, but then don't have the relationships that would help with sales. If you build relationships with those who have an compatible existing audience and you have a systematic way of doing that, you dramatically can expand your impact. Let's take a moment to discuss how to accomplish that. What does the process look like? Usually the first thing you want to have is a platform — a podcast — where you can invite people to participate.

The way to do this is by strategically choosing your guests. Consider having two *buckets*, and the first bucket is going to be potential clients. These are people with whom you might want to do business, but may be strategic clients that would be difficult to reach otherwise. Usually, that's a minority of guests. It's a great way to get in front of potential clients and create business directly. The other group consists of those who can promote you. These are other business owners who have a network full of people of interest to you. As you begin to identify this group, it all starts falling into place. You can send a simple email with little convincing. Just communicate that you have a podcast, it has an established audience, we talk about these important topics, and we'd love to have you as a guest — would you be interested?

You'd be shocked how easy it is to get somebody to say yes. For example, a client of mine who hadn't yet launched their podcast, decided they wanted to invite Tony Horton as a guest. Tony Horton is an entrepreneur in the fitness industry and started a program called P90x, which has been around for 20-plus years and is extremely successful. Tony runs a big company and is a celebrity in the fitness community. My client works in the financial services industry and lives in the Midwest. He didn't have anything in place beyond an idea for his podcast. Yet he reached out to Tony Horton, expressing his admiration and inviting Tony to be on the show. There would be no other way to have a conversation with a man like Tony, but running a podcast opens many doors. It's very easy to get that "yes" — and it leads to unbelievable experiences.

Tony Horton Podcast Interview

By and large, it's simple to have these conversations that allow you to start forming these relationships. It's powerful. The way to turn these opportunities to collaborate further and promote your book also is simple. Think of it this way — you are interested in the other person, so you just interview them, but once the recording is off, you continue the conversation. You can ask where they are going, what the future looks like for them, or their plans for their business in the next three years. Another great question is asking about their long-term goals. The most important part is just listen, *genuinely* listen, because you want to understand this person and where they are going. That's when you can add value.

Three Ways to Add Value

1 If they have a goal your business can help support, let them know you have some ideas for their company. For example, if they said they are wanting to achieve a specific goal, you can explain how your business can help them obtain that goal faster, cheaper, and easier. You'll ask if they're interested in having a conversation about that — and guess what they're going to say? Yes.

2 The second way to add value is by helping them with connections. Since you have a podcast and you're interviewing great guests, these business leaders, whether in your community or international business leaders, you're building relationships and a very strong network. Those connections can then be an asset to your other guests. You can connect people now within this community of your guests.

3 The last way to demonstrate value is by sharing your book to help grow connections. Let your guest know you've got a large network you're nurturing. You wrote a book, and it might be a value to the people in their network. A little side note — if you've been strategic about who you're inviting, you already know they have the right audience for you. You know that the audience would benefit from your book.

You offer to give it to their audience as a gift. It gives you a great way to nurture your audience and give them value. Let them know that you normally SELL the book, but would love to GIVE it to their audience. When you ask if they would be open to doing that, the majority of the time they say yes. It's easy *and* an authentic thing to do. You're looking for ways to genuinely add value.

We want to peel back the curtain a bit again and give you an example of how we're applying this today. We showed you what I did with my first book. We've learned some things since then, and we want to share with you the strategy that we're using now. This is something that you'll be able to take and put directly into your business. What we'll be talking about here is using my book, *Podcast Prospecting*.

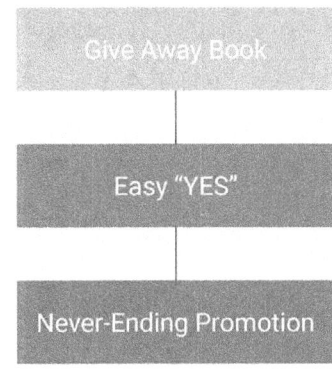

Current Promo-Giveaway – "Yes" – Never-Ending Promotion

The first important part of the strategy is to give the book away. It's interesting. I had a client a couple years ago who had written an amazing book, particularly for his field. It was probably one of the leading thought pieces in this field. Unfortunately, he put it out there and he priced it on Amazon at like 80 bucks. It was worth every bit of that and more to the right business, but he got frustrated, because he hardly sold any. Very few people understood it. It wasn't driving any business results for him. A big mistake that often is made is that people give the book away, but they didn't really give it away. For example, I was running one of those penny plus shipping offers where you could buy the book for 18 dollars on Amazon, but I'd send you a paperback if you pay me a penny and cover the shipping cost to buy direct from me. I did that for about 18 months. During that time, I sold about five thousand books. It was a lot of work. And it wasn't free to do that.

At the time, I was running Facebook ads with affiliate partners who were sharing it. It was hard to get an affiliate partner to share, because they weren't giving a gift, they were just trying to get them to pitch someone on buying a book from them. We were barely breaking even and were about three dollars negative on each book. Unless you're going to sell millions of copies — and that's not likely to happen unless you've got the audience already to support that — it's not worth it. If you *do* have that kind of audience, you wouldn't be reading this book.

Give Your Book Away

Please give the book away. We know, it sounds counterproductive, but trust us, it's going to be worth more to you to give it away. Of course, you'll still have it for sale on Amazon or your website, but you'll find there is far more value in *gifting* your book than *waiting* for sales to happen. This creates an extremely easy *Yes*. For all partnerships that you're developing through your podcast, they're going to be more inclined to say yes and work with you. It creates a positive image of you and your company. Almost any audience will appreciate it if you do that. By these partners saying yes, they also are saying, I'm willing to refer you to everyone I know — via your book.

Consider asking your strategic partners the following questions: Who do you know that needs some consulting help with referrals? Do you have any clients or contacts that need help? You would be lucky to get one or two responses out of our 15 to 20 people total. Doesn't sound very lucrative, right? That's because it isn't. It comes across pushy and like your typical sales pitch. Instead you can offer them a simple way to share your wisdom and knowledge if it's packaged in the form of a book. Something that all those in their network would see as a really valuable gift. Something that even the strategic partner themselves would see as valuable to give away. It is easy to get them to say yes. It's critical that you shift your mindset in how you approach strategic partners and potential clients. It's a struggle for a lot of authors. And we won't lie, it's going to hold you back. So, give the book away. Make it an easy *yes*. You want to create the ability to have a never-ending promotion.

A huge mistake that we often see is that the author only has a book-launch plan. They fail to create a marketing plan after the book is published. They'll have partners lined up for the launch and a set schedule for pre-marketing, so much so that they'll get so exhausted through the process that they won't have a plan to address post book release. They're overwhelmed from their journey, neglecting to figure out how they were going to flourish during the rest of their publication period. You may see a big influx of prospects for about two or three months following the launch, which are very high level. That's when an odd phase starts to set in. Without a podcast as a steady way to promote your book, you're likely to resort to Facebook ads and other promotional options, such as Instagram ads or Amazon ads. Where would you be if you had an ongoing plan to use the book to drive leads to land clients?

That's why we're writing this book, so we can talk about the combination of a book and a podcast. The book is the object that allows you to package your expertise and give it away. You must have that, because it's going to allow you to really scale your lead generation. You're not going to have to educate every prospect one by one. How is that possible? Your book is going to do it for you. It's also going to tell you more than you thought possible about your prospects. Those who requested the book are just like everyone else — we all judge books by their covers, particularly the titles and subtitles. If you have the right title and the subtitle that speaks to the people you're trying to attract, you're going to get great leads from that alone. All you need now is a way to constantly create and build relationships with people who already have built the right audience for you. Building the right audience sounds like a lot of work, but it doesn't need to be with a podcast and strategic networking. We could go so far as to say you don't need to build an audience at all. All you *need* to do is give your strategic partners an opportunity to give that audience a gift — *your book*!

The Exponential Network Strategy book

Mistakes happen, though. Especially when you're not sure what to do or where to start. An example of mine comes from one of my failures between my first and fourth book. I'll tell you a little secret about my second book entitled, *The Exponential Network Strategy*. It's largely the same topic as the new book *Podcast Prospecting*. I wrote the book with new content making it more up to date and relevant.

Unfortunately, *The Exponential Network Strategy* didn't achieve the success and lead generation I anticipated. You know why? Because, the title *sucks*. It's terrible. Nobody knows what the exponential network strategy is. It was a little too cute and wasn't very marketable. I don't want you to make that mistake. In December, I realized that I needed to change it up, because I simply was not generating the leads I was seeking. It was a learning curve and mistakes were made, but it led to greater understanding of how titles and subtitles can work to your benefit. I came back and decided that it needed to have a relevant word in the title, which in this case was *Podcast*. The lead you want is someone who already is familiar with your book's message. In this case, the reader would have the thought, "Hmm, I might want a podcast one day." We don't care where they are in the decision-making process, we just need them to have that one defining thought. The mere fact that they raised a hand and requested a book that is entitled *Podcast Prospecting*, tells me this is a potential client for me. They've already had the key thought we want them to have, so we don't need to convince them about that part.

It's time for the next step — it's going to be a whole lot easier now that you have the right kind of leads! Now you can put all your energy and focus on the more interesting part and it makes everything so much easier.

My book, *Podcast Prospecting*, had been out for about a week. At the time, I had around 150 strategic partners that were in the process of working through plans to help promote the book. The strategic partners were people that I had interviewed on my podcast over a three-year period. In those three short years, I created 150 relationships. That's a powerful network — all thanks to my podcast.

What happened in only a couple of weeks as I launched the book, my very first partner shared the book with his list on February 21. On February 24, I sent two emails out to my list. Around that same time, I also was featured as a guest on *The Duct Tape Marketing Podcast*. It's managed by a brilliant guy named John Jantsch, and his books are amazing. He has probably one of the oldest podcasts in the business, and one of the biggest podcast audiences as well. His audience opens a new generation of leads, and these leads are happy! What does that mean? Well, they're happy, because they just received a free book on a topic in which they're interested, ultimately landing new clients.

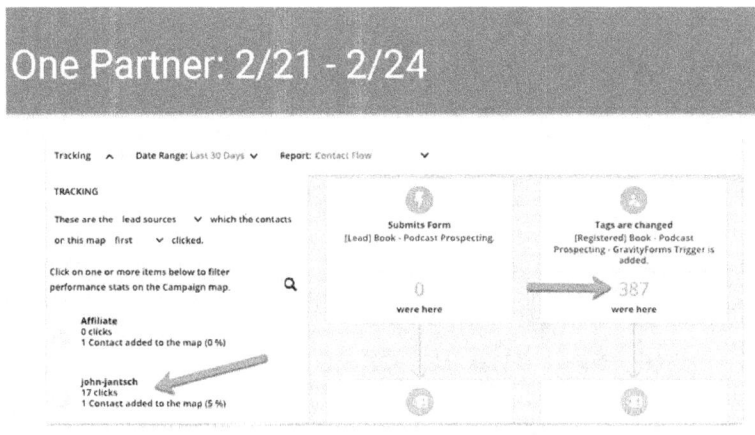

Strategic Partnership numbers: 2/21-2/24

Call to Action

It's important to have a call to action at the beginning and end of your book or podcast. It can be as simple as saying that you have a whole team standing by ready to assist if the reader or listener, is seeking your services. Make it personal and connect with the reader. Let them know how they can reach out to you, even if it's just to ask questions and see how your business works. Before you know it, you'll be landing new clients and getting your first payment from them!

The call to action might include a landing page or opt-in form that includes a field for the name and email. In return for their name and email, you may provide a bonus PDF, audio, or video as a bonus. Your call to action also may be for them to call you by asking them to text their name and email to opt-in to your autoresponder. No matter what call to action you choose, don't forget to include it at the beginning *and* end of the podcast or book.

Power of a Book

That's the power of having a book. That's the power of having the ability to create these strategic partners. You're not left to run ads or hoping that SEO is going to work. It puts you back in control of your lead generation and your marketing. It's a very powerful strategy.

Questions to ask yourself:

    1. When should I start my podcast?
    2. Who should I invite as a guest?

3. How many listeners do I need to be successful?
4. What's the biggest reason authors fail?
5. Is the podcast strategy just good at the launch?
6. Is it better to promote my book on other podcasts or host my own?
7. All this sounds great, but how could it go wrong?

3

Writing the Book That Writes Itself

— Melanie Johnson

Easy Steps to Writing a Book!

You've probably heard it said, or perhaps even said it yourself, "I should write a book about that!"

A lot of people want to write a book. Eighty percent of people say they want to write a book. Many only think about writing a book, with only one percent actually following through. The question is, *What stops them?*

One simple answer is: fear, exhaustion, high standards (which is basically fear of failure), Imposter Syndrome (fear of rejection), perfectionism (fear of not being good enough), busyness (fear of not having enough time), laziness (really fear in sheep's clothing?), lack of structure (fear of not knowing how to start), and did I mention *fear?*

Brené Brown

Writing a book opens you up to be critiqued by friends, family, readers, and competitors. A great video we share with all our authors when they go through our VIP Book Creation Day is Brené Brown's TED Talk, *The Power of Vulnerability*.

Internationally acclaimed researcher, author, and speaker Brené Brown, a research professor at the University of Houston, is bringing her influence and thought leadership to The University of Texas at Austin to facilitate a new leadership training program centered around courage, trust, and vulnerability. As a visiting professor of management at the McCombs School of Business, "You don't have to be a great writer to get started, but to be great, you have to start!"

Think of all the things that might be holding you back — we are going to overcome some of those things that may be blocking you right now. First, you don't need to be a writer to write a book. Sounds crazy, right? It is not. My son always gets on my case, because I say, "I'm not really a writer." My son says, "Don't say that! You own a publishing company. Don't say that you're not a writer." But I am not that comfortable with writing. I'm not the type to go into what they call "the writing cave" and churn out words as if it is natural. In fact, it is very far from natural for me. I get stuck all the time while at my computer writing, all while lamenting, "How do I get the words I want to say typed into my word document, the way I want to say it? The idea doesn't read as well as it sounded in my head."

It is okay to feel this way. We have a plethora of tools and processes that we are going to go through that will help you write a book. You are going to learn how to get your book done quickly. You may not even have to write one word of it. Wouldn't that be cool?

Why Publish a Book — Now!

The previous chapters addressed the power of a book and a podcast, and how they can increase your success. Now we're going to dive in a little bit deeper.

Some of you do not know where to start. After all, writing a book can seem incredibly daunting. We have clients — some who signed on this week — and the ideas just kept rolling around in their head. They thought, *'Maybe I should write about this. Maybe I should write about that.'* They just cannot get to that starting point. That's what is stopping them from starting to write a book.

We are going to tackle that initial fear — the doubt you have in yourself. You may be thinking, *'What if I'm not a writer? How can I possibly write a book?'* Remember, your book becomes your business card that speaks volumes, *pun intended.*

One of our mentors, Mike Koenigs, showed us how to make the next big thing happen. Mike is a 16-time #1 bestselling author. Quite a few years ago he started *The Digital Café*, a podcast show where he interviewed experts and talked about digital marketing. Mike owned one of the world's first interactive digital marketing agencies serving companies including BMW, General Mills, Sony, Columbia/Tristar, 20th Century Fox, Carlson Companies, AT&T, Blue Cross/Blue Shield, 3M, Domino's Pizza and dozens of other large brands, and in '99 sold to Campbell Mithun Esty, a subsidiary of the publicly traded Interpublic Group (IPG).

Mike Koenigs

Then in 2003, he produced, *Everything You Should Know About Publishing, Publicity, Promotion and Building a Platform*, a big-ticket information product with the legendary Arielle Ford — long-time publicist for Deepak Chopra and responsible for placing some of the biggest authors on Oprah. Arielle represented 11 *NY Times* bestselling authors, including Deepak Chopra, Wayne Dyer, Neal Donald Walsh, Jack Canfield, Mark Victor Hansen, Debbie Ford, Louise Hay, Don Miguel Ruiz, Gary Zukav, Dean Ornish, Joan Borysenko, Jorge Cruise, and Lynne Twist. The course helped thousands of people start and build their author platforms — and one of our earliest customers was Tim Ferriss before he published *The Four-Hour Work Week*. In 2004 Mike went on to release, *The Internet Infomercial Toolkit*, in 2008 he launched the *Instant Customer*, in 2009 he launched *Main Street Marketing Machines*, in 2015 *Podcasting*

Authorized launched *The Mike Koenigs Show and Podcast*, and in 2016 *You Everywhere Now Product Suite*.

By chance, he found himself staring out the port side of a plane one day and noticed Richard Dreyfuss sitting in the first-class section. For those of us old enough to know the actor, Richard Dreyfuss is an American actor best known for starring in popular films between the 1970s and 1990s, including *American Graffiti, Jaws, Stand by Me, Close Encounters of the Third Kind, Down and Out in Beverly Hills, The Goodbye Girl, Tin Men, Stake-out, Always,* and *What About Bob?*

When Mike got off the plane, he realized they were both stuck in a short layover in a long terminal. After Googling around, Mike discovered Richard had a non-profit foundation, Prioritizing Civics Education — "Teach our kids how to run our country before they are called upon to run our country... if we don't, someone else will run our country," TheDreyfussInitiative.org. The Dreyfuss Civics Initiative is a non-profit, non-partisan organization that aims to revive the teaching of civics in American public education to empower future generations with the critical-thinking skills they need to fulfill the vast potential of American citizenship. Richard had been actively searching for new money.

Richard Dreyfuss and Mike Koenigs on set at the Digital Café

In the terminal, sitting at the gates waiting for the next big thing to happen, Mike approached Richard Dreyfuss and expressed what a big fan he was and handed him a copy of his book with the section marked on how to raise money for a charity. Mike took this opportunity, and boldly signed the book for him. As time went by and the bustling life of an airport terminal squirrel, walking around the carousel, visiting restrooms, eating, duty-free shopping, before re-boarding the plane, Richard went up to Mike and said, "I love this, you're going to be my new best friend. Where are you sitting? Let's upgrade you to first-class, because I want you to sit next to me. I want to know everything you know."

The next thing you know, they had a working agreement between one another. He and Richard became friends, and Mike interviewed him on his podcast, *The Mike Koenigs Show and Podcast*, and the Dreyfuss Foundation became a new client.

That's how you use your book as a business card. Business cards are lost and thrown away. They become obsolete and hardly memorable, and quickly the person forgets why he has your card in his pocket in the first place. However, a book is a different story, *more puns*. It never gets thrown away and it becomes *the* most memorable business card you can hand a person, and because of this, you're going to get more clients.

As we touched on earlier, a book can help your business and allow you to gain more clients and leads. You can use it for free to give away to different people. You can leverage the content on your social media, you can give it away as a gift, you can send it to an entire office at one time, there are endless ways a book can benefit your business. There is nothing else that establishes your credibility like a book.

It's one of the oldest tools of the trade — books have been around forever. Take a moment to *really* think about it. Do you connect with people? Of course, but it is nothing like you would with a book. People are still in awe when you tell them you are an author. They are instantly impressed with that, and your credibility shoots through the roof. All of this because you took the time to compress all your knowledge and write it down in one place, and then shared it with the world. It makes you stand out in your industry.

Imagine you are searching for a web designer, and while comparing options, you notice one of them has a bestselling book. Not only will you have the option to look through their book, but you are going to know that this person is an expert that can be trusted. Take this a step further. We want you to think about your industry. What is your niche? Imagine all that compiled into a book. Who else in your industry has a book? Which author in your industry is a number one bestseller? It's the bestseller status of your book that's going to make you stand out. Now think about it, you have a book, and your competitor does not. Not only that, but you are giving that book away for free. People are thumbing through it, while the competitor may simply be a name or webpage they visited.

People want to work with an expert. They do not want to work with just anyone. Money matters. Time matters. Quality and expertise matter. You know those commercials that are airing, and it's about a dentist or doctor, claiming their credibility and achievements. If you are looking for someone in that field, you are going to want to work with them. They are clearly the top in their field. When you have a bestselling book, it sets you up as that expert, and it showcases your brand. The bestseller sticker on the cover is beautiful. Stamped on your book is a title that sets you apart and attracts attention — #1 BESTSELLING AUTHOR. It is an extension of your brand. Everything inside the book is an extension of your brand. You are going to be able to use it as the ultimate marketing tool.

For example, when you have your book, you're putting all that content together, you're going to have enough social media content in there for years to come — it may even be endless. We tell our clients to include quotes in their book, so they can use it as social media content. You can use the themes of your chapters, or you can read from your book in a live video. The possibilities are limitless! You even can send it to different experts or offer it to them as a gift for their clients! We successfully held a contest with one of our books. We have story-starter books with prompts in them — *How to Write Your Life Story and Leave a Legacy,* and *How to Write Your Story of Accomplishment and Success,* both available on Amazon. Each book offers 50-plus questions to help start your story. We took those and we created a book-writing challenge, using the entire content of the book. Every week, we sent out a question. And, that's just one example. There is a multitude of ways you can use your book to create content and market yourself. You are going to get media attention, you're going to create new relationships, generate quality leads, and discover new clients!

One story we love is from Marilynn Barber, one of our authors. She's a wardrobe consultant, and her book is: *Dress Like You Mean Business.*

Dress Like You Mean Business book

One day in 2016, she commented on a newscaster's Facebook post. The newscaster noticed she had this book and she said, "Oh my gosh, I would love to have you come on our television station and talk about the strategy of the political candidate's wardrobe, what they're wearing, and what that says about them."

She did it and then immediately got a gig on ABC News in the media — not even just an interview — she was put on there as an expert. They loved her *so* much throughout the campaign that they had her on as a regular segment for what the candidates were wearing. Can you imagine now if she did not have her book? Nothing would have set her apart and that would have never *ever* happened. abc13.com/1588153

Marilynn Barber on ABC in the *Dress Like You Mean Business* Segment

Your book is going to last forever. When your book goes up for sale on Amazon and is published everywhere, even if you decide to take it off, it stays up there forever, your book will still be up there, even if people can't buy it. Usually, it's still for sale by third-party sellers. Your book lasts forever!

Repurpose Your Content

Getting into the nitty-gritty of what you're *really* here for — how to write a book. One of our favorite ways to start writing a book is by repurposing your content. So many people ask where to start — they have no idea where to even begin. Sure, they have ideas, and they know the type of content they want to write, but they are not sure how to collect that all into a book. So, start with what you already have!

The Perfect Example

We have an author who is saying, "I don't know if I should write about this or if I should write about that." Turns out, he has speeches he can use. He holds probably three to four speeches a month, and always is writing new speeches. Because of this, he has an entire library of speeches that he has written. The great part about that? All the speeches could be distilled together into a book. Do you have blogs that you have written? Do you have newsletters that you distribute? Or, maybe you have a podcast? That brings us to where we started — there is a significant benefit to having a podcast.

Diving into repurposing a bit more, this is just another example. The Minimalists, Joshua Fields Millburn and Ryan Nicodemus, started writing blog posts, they turned the blog posts right into a book, *Minimalism*, and then the book became a movie on Netflix. Think about that, content that just started with blog articles that turned into a book, and ultimately turned into a movie. Did they have to do more work? Really *no*, very little. With a book and a movie, they had a plethora of content to use.

The Minimalists

This is true for podcasts, too! Take a look at Tim Ferris, who published *Tools of the Titans*. He is also the author of *The Four-Hour Work Week*. He used his podcast, and he took all his shows and put them together and made a book out of it. It's a common, helpful method for writing a book. In fact, we used it too! We've had a podcast going for almost five years now. In the first year of our podcast, we took the first 32 episodes and turned them into a book. The title of that book is: *The Book Writing Bible*. It's just that easy!

Maybe you do not have a podcast yet, and that sounds like another daunting task to begin, it's not. It is simply having a conversation — and we do that all the time. If you are going to start your podcast and create content that way, be strategic! Think about what you want to write about. Create an outline of ideas, and then each podcast is part of that chapter. You could even make each podcast a whole chapter, or maybe just a section of the chapter. When you start with your podcast, have a whole plan of episodes already laid out of what you want the topics to be, what it is about the business that you want featured in your book. This is extremely beneficial. Whatever it is, it must be specific to *your* business. Think about who you are trying to attract, the kind of clients you'd like to attract. If you already have a flyer that you're using, or you have a Facebook ad that you're running adjust it to target your ideal client and to get them to come into your funnel. That is what your book needs to look like!

A Few Tips on Your Book Content

What many authors forget to do is that they forget to have a call to action in their book. We are going to tell you right now in the beginning, you need to have a method where they can reach you and can get more information — something they can opt into. You want to be able to capture their email address and their contact information. Because when people buy your book online, they're not giving you that information from Amazon or Barnes and Noble. It cannot be emphasized enough how important it is that you put a call to action in the beginning and the end of the book. Why do we say it in the beginning? Because even if someone doesn't buy your book, Amazon looks inside the book, gives you a preview of the first few pages of your book, this way readers can see where to contact you and opt in for that extra special thing that you're giving away with the book. In the Kindle version of look inside the book, the link is clickable, your readers can click and opt in, without ever having bought your book.

Become an Expert — Interview Experts

Another great way to create and repurpose content is by interviewing experts. For example, we're going to start with a friend of ours, Justine. Justine was going through a divorce and was having a terrible time trying to figure out what to do to find a great attorney. She interviewed some and she ended up with a bad one and had to change to another one. Her divorce was a long process and she knew she hadn't chosen the right lawyer for her. Because of this experience, she came up with the idea to help other women, so they didn't have to suffer through the same process that she did when trying to find a great lawyer. However, she didn't feel like she was an expert in that field. So, she went out and interviewed all the top divorce lawyers in her city. She had them pay her a fee to be interviewed on her podcast, and then it was transcribed into the book. This paid for her publishing and she made a profit on the book before it was even published. Her book was published a short time after she interviewed the attorneys. They were all very happy to be featured in the book and on the podcast. Her title is on Amazon: *LAWYER UP!: 7 Step Guide to Help You Find the Right Attorney for YOUR Needs.*

You may not be an expert yet, but you can interview other people to *become* the expert. Most know Tony

Robbins, a very famous icon. His book *Money Masters* takes content from different financial people as clients of his. It was when we went through the market crash of 2008-2009 that inspired him. A few years after that, he wrote this book. And he went and interviewed all the people that were his clients and other experts he knew in this field to share all the advice that they had. Was Tony the expert? No, he wasn't the expert. Of course, he knew things and he interjected things, but really, it was all the other experts he interviewed. Now think about what other experts you could interview to create a book. Or think about potential dream clients you could interview to be in the book. They may be in a similar or complementary field. There are limitless options!

Returning to our example, Justine wasn't a lawyer and didn't know anything about being a lawyer, but maybe she was going to be a consultant *to* lawyers. So, she could ask to interview these lawyers, get in front of them, and get her foot in the door by asking them to participate in her book. You can do the same! There are other ways you could find strategic partners who you want to be in your book, or you could find people who are in the niche you're trying to attract.

Okay, at this point some of you may say, "Oh, my gosh, I have all this down, but to sit and write? It would just be such a pain. I have all the topics for my chapters. I have things that I want to talk about, but I can't possibly write this down." You could talk to your best friend about those ideas, right? Or if you're at a dinner party, you could just chat away about it without a second thought. So why don't you sit down with someone and have them interview you and ask you about those things about your business? It's that simple! Again, if you plan ahead then all that content can be gathered while they're interviewing you. You can record it and easily have the interview transcribed.

Another example is Jay Lucas. He was one of those types — you know the ones who have a plan, schedule, and to-do list for absolutely everything. He had a great plan, too. He rented a studio and asked someone he knew with a media background to interview him. They transcribed all the interviews and created his book. However, in addition to that, there's also video footage of the interviews. Now he has the video leverage, as well as all the content for his book. It's a two-for-one. You have videos that you can post on Facebook or YouTube, you can upload to your website, or you can distribute as email with snippets of the interview to promote your book and business.

Someone Interviews You!

Another way to write your book fast is to have someone interview you. You might be thinking that sounds intimidating — and that's reasonable! We all have different boundaries, limits, and comfort levels. Thankfully we live in the age of technology and artificial intelligence offers a great way that you can do it all by yourself. You could literally be sitting in your closet, in your car, or hanging out at the gym and you can talk your book into existence. One of our favorite options to do this is the app Evernote, but you can also use the Notes feature or the Voice app on your phone. Another great option is Otter.ai — we *love* Otter! It will record in real time what you're saying, and you'll have an audio recording of it. Out of all these, we find that it has the best transcription. Of course, all have a few little glitches here and there. A helpful tip to allow you to get the most accurate transcription is you want to be as close to the microphone as possible. After you talk out your book, you have everything transcribed. Then you can hire an editor or ghostwriter to fix it up.

Use A.I.

Artificial Intelligence (A.I.)

Think about it this way, we often do our best thinking at seemingly random times. You might do your best thinking when you're on the treadmill or working out and sometimes when you're in the car sitting at a light, you find yourself hit with inspiration. You can just turn on one of these apps and start talking. If you're on a long drive on the freeway and just start talking it out, during that two- or three-hour drive, you can have your whole book talked out in that time. It can take you 30 days, or less to have your whole book written simply by recording yourself. *It doesn't have to take years to write your book. It can be captured in a matter of hours!*

Interview Yourself on Camera

Another way to write a book is you can video yourself. You can capture different clips and video yourself talking about your services and products. Once you have that, you can go back and figure out the order and have it transcribed. It's written for you with little effort!

Pros and Cons

If you're thinking you don't know *what* to write or *how* to create your content *still*, there's an easy solution. One of our favorite writing styles is to do pros and cons, as well as do's and don'ts. For an example, the pros and cons of a topic, such as having a podcast. You take this idea and say, "here are the top pros and cons of having a podcast." Why should you have a podcast, and what are the do's and don'ts when you're looking for starting one. The do's and don'ts for real estate, the do's and don'ts for digital marketing. Whatever your topic may be, if you pick the top 10 do's or the top 10 don'ts, that is a book right there. It sounds easy because it is! If you're stuck, do that! This will give you a platform for creating content, whether by writing or recording and transcribing.

The 10x3x3 Writing Formula

- Top 10 FAQ
- Top 10 SAQ
- 1-3 Short Stories
- 3 points for each story

The 10x3x3 writing formula

There is another formula we use, it's really great, and beyond simple! It's called the 10x3x3. Even if you took only 10 minutes and worked on this formula, we guarantee you would have more than 10 of each of these. So, what exactly is this formula?

People get the most frequently asked questions on your expertise, your service, product, or niche all the time. You're getting these questions over and over again. Ask yourself — what are the most frequently asked questions you get all the time? Then think of what we call the: "Should Ask Questions" or SAQs. These are the questions that if they knew what you knew they should be asking. We'll use podcasting as an example again. A common question might be, "how hard is it to be a podcaster?" At that point you would say, "what you should be asking is how many clients I can get if I had a podcast." Write down as many SAQs as you can!

Then after you have your FAQs and SAQs, we want you to think about one to three stories for each of those questions. The stories can be about an experience you had for yourself, about a friend, or about something you heard on the news. It doesn't even need to be somebody you know — it could be a story shared with you about something. You just want to have a story that goes with it. We want you to have a point that explains what this means for the reader after the question and the stories. Here is a great illustration. We love using church as an example — at least everyone has gone once or twice in their life, *at least*. And some people are regular churchgoers. Usually a minister starts with the Scripture, and then he gives some real-life stories of how that scripture is illustrated, right? He talks about it, they go into the story, and then they ask — *What does this mean for you?*

How can you relate this to your life? What is the point of this?

This is the 10x3x3 writing formula for your chapters; you want to start with a transformational story, talk about the question that it's solving, and then a point that illustrates how it relates to the reader and how they can use this lesson to improve business or other areas of their life.

Regardless of your method, when you're trying to research ideas for your book, we want you simply to think about your business, how you can use the information you already have and repurpose what you already have created.

You're Not Recreating the Wheel

Think about what sells your business to other people and align yourself as the expert in that field. What is it going to take to convince the reader that *you* are the expert. When they read your book, they should be thinking, "Wow, they know everything about this topic! I should hire them to do this."

Not only that, but you want them to learn something. If they learned something, then this is the person to hire if I were to do that.

The easiest way that we're telling you to do this — to create a book and content — is to come up with a podcast. Once you have a podcast, you have the content of your book, and then you can publish the book and use it over and over again. The most important takeaway here is to tell your story and get it out there. Take that little bit of time, take those few hours — it's really that easy to create your book by drafting the outline, use the Otter app, otter.ai get your transcription edited, and then you have a book you can use for a lifetime!

4

PUBLISH YOUR BOOK!

— Melanie Johnson

"Your personal brand is a promise to your clients... a promise of quality, consistency, competency, and reliability."

— Jason Hartman, author of Become the Brand of Choice

When it's time to create your book, make sure that your brand is represented. You want to build the same brand across all social media platforms. Your branding may include a headshot, three to five colors, fonts, and other pictures. Your book and your website need brand consistency. If your book and your website are entirely different, it looks like it's two different companies or individuals. There are several ways in which to make sure your brand is telling the same story throughout all your social media platforms, website, and book. Branding consistency will ensure that your book is marketable.

A Winning Title

The title and subtitle are vital in developing your brand. It's also essential to creating a book that can be successfully marketed. As much as we want to think everyone's going to read every page of our book, that's not always the case. If it is — you're lucky. We *really* do judge a book by the cover, and the title is part of the cover.

A winning title includes the following formula:
This book is for _____ (audience) who has/have _____ (problem) so that you can _____ (get a benefit, result, outcome, cure)...

Book Title Samples

The following are a few of my favorite titles that include this formula and are some of the best, most effective business books ever written. *Notice how the titles reflect the above criteria*!

> *The 4-Hour Work Week: Escape 9-5, Live Anywhere and Join the New Rich*
> By Tim Ferriss

- *The 7 Habits of Highly Effective People*
  By Stephen R. Covey

- *The 22 Immutable Laws of Marketing: Violate Them at Your Own Risk!*
  By Al Ries and Jack Trout

- *Drive: The Surprising Truth About What Motivates Us*
  By Daniel Pink

- *The E-Myth: Why Most Small Businesses Don't Work and What to Do About it*
  By Michael Gerber

- *The Essential Drucker: The Best of Sixty Years of Peter Drucker's Essential Writings on Management*
  By Peter Drucker

- *First, Break all the Rules: What the World's Greatest Managers Do Differently*
  By Marcus Buckingham and Curt Coffman

- *Flow: The Psychology of Optimal Experience*
  By Mihaly Csikzentmihalyi

- *Good to Great: Why Some Companies Make the Leap... and Others Don't*
  By Jim Collins

- *Influence: The Psychology of Persuasion*
  By Robert Cialdini, PhD

- *Out of the Crisis*
  By W. Edwards Deming

- *In Search of Excellence: Lessons from America's Best-Run Companies*
  By Thomas Peters, Robert H. Waterman

- *Getting Things Done: The Art of Stress-Free Productivity*
  By David Allen

- *How to Win Friends and Influence People*
  By Dale Carnegie

- *Think and Grow Rich*
  By Napoleon Hill

- *The Tipping Point: How Little Things Can Make a Big Difference*
  By Malcolm Gladwell

- *Unlimited Power: The New Science of Personal Achievement*
  By Anthony Robbins

Book Cover

Your book cover is very important. Not only does it need to look good on a bookshelf, but it needs to stand out as a small one-inch icon online. The Amazon app and website will feature your book as a small icon. It is important that your book cover has contrast. If the book is white with small letters it will not stand out same if it's dark with dark letters, no one will be able to read it. You want a book that stands out. Go to Amazon and search a topic of your choice in the book category. Notice the icons. Which book covers stand out to you? These are the book covers you will want to model. You also can peruse an airport book stand. Which book covers stand out the most? How is the title positioned?

I have a book that was given to me the other day, I set it on my nightstand. It has the author's picture on the cover, which is great, because he's kind of well known. Every night before going to bed, I keep staring at his face on the book cover. Have I read the book yet? No, I have not. I know who this guy is. I know what he can offer, and I see his book every night. He is top of my mind each night. I say to myself, *'I really need to take time to read that book.'* The moral of the story? GET OVER YOURSELF! Perfect is perfect enough. Get your book out there, whether you think you're ready or not. You want your book on someone's nightstand, creating a lasting impression.

We have a potential client that has been wanting to work with us for two years. But every time we circle back to him, he's not quite ready. Maybe he just wants to edit the manuscript one more time. "I just feel like I need to do it one more time." Think about it, how much revenue could he have generated in the last two years if he had published his book? Keep in mind, when you publish your book, if you find minor grammar mistakes, or you find something you wish you could have written differently — guess what? You can make the changes, if you self-publish, you can just re-submit the edited version. We probably have typos in this book. If you see them, email us and let us know. We'd appreciate it.

So again, we repeat: GET OVER YOURSELF!

> *"You don't need to be great to get started. But to be great, you have to start."*
>
> — *Les Brown*

The most important thing is that you get it done and get it out there. Create a podcast to get your content written. Ask somebody to interview you. Capture that content and spin it into a book. Get it published and available to the public.

You still may be hesitant. Isn't the whole reason to publish a book is so people will read it? Sure, we'd love for everyone to read our book. We actually signed a client, who told us on our first call together that he had a copy of my book. He got it when we launched our podcast in 2015. He said he ordered an eBook version and then the paperback. He had the paperback sitting on his nightstand. How often do you take a book to bed with you or place it in your room? A book is the only marketing tool that can follow your client to the bedroom, throughout their home, or anywhere for that matter. The book plants a seed, unlike the traditional business card.

Going back to our story about our client. He never opened the book, but he said he finally just had to call. He expressed his need for the content in the book, but he wasn't going to read it. That's typical. They intend to read it. They may move it to the bedroom or near their favorite chair. They may carry it around with them. However, if you send them a flyer or a card or something like that, it doesn't do that. It gets thrown away. Emails, Facebook advertisements, and other marketing options are temporary. A book has longevity, and it does something to the subconscious. When you look at it over and over again, it does something. You can't quantify that. It's beyond money. A book will give value that will last for years and years.

Book Marketing and Promotions

You might be familiar with Dan Sullivan. He recently started writing short books and is publishing a book every quarter. There is a certain brilliance about putting out a book every quarter or putting out books frequently. During a conversation at a *Mastermind* with Dan Kennedy. He was talking about his books and where he was at this point in his career. He was going back and resurrecting books that he'd published maybe a decade before and adding a couple of new chapters in them. Then he would publish a second edition or an entirely new version of the book. His goal was to launch two or three books a year. The reason for this was that he wanted to always have something to promote.

Dan Sullivan

It's so much easier for us to promote a book for all the reasons that we've talked about here. You can get strategic partners that are there to help you promote it. You don't need to create as many books as Sullivan with one book a quarter, which is probably a bit overkill for most people. You just really need one good one. However, what he does is he repurposes them in a lot of ways. He'll actually have someone on his team interview him; instead of doing a traditional audiobook, they interview him. This is how they get the book content. They start with an outline of the interview. Then they turn the interview into an audiobook. They also video the interview so that there's a video version of it, as well. They take the content and turn it into a scorecard. So, you can grade how you're doing in that area of your business. Then of course, the whole thing gets written by someone other than Dan and turned into a book. It's brilliant. It's a fantastic way to get a book out there!

Look how much media he created out of that! He doesn't necessarily have to promote himself; the book is doing it for him. It's a great way to start a conversation with potential clients. If you need to follow up with potential clients, then instead of asking if they want your product or service, let them know you have a new book out. Ask them if they would like a free copy! It's just a great way to reconnect and start a conversation.

You want to talk about a referral tool? Books. Books are the best marketing tool to get you referrals. About once or twice a year I order about 100-250 books. I order them at the wholesale price, to give them out to clients and partners. When you have strategic partners, you can give them copies of your book to hand out to prospective clients. That's the power of having the right book. I have clients who have secured many new clients of their own by doing this.

If you have been thinking about writing a book, it's time to get off the fence. It's time to use your book as a marketing tool and profit from your book.

5

BOOK AND PODCAST BEST PRACTICES

— Jenn Foster

How to Record a Podcast

For our podcast, *Elite Expert Insider,* we record our interviews using video on Zoom. Zoom video conferencing can record using the microphone and speakers built right into your desktop. You also could plug in an external microphone and headphones to improve the audio quality. Zoom can record your interview and store the audio and video file on the cloud or on your computer.

You could record your podcast using other methods. A few ways would be using audio editing software like Garageband, Logic Pro, Adobe Audition, or Audacity. We use the audio to produce our podcast, but video is an option for those who are comfortable with it. Regardless of your method to creating a podcast, you get the best results from the audio. You can even take a version of it and put it on YouTube. You could create a video using the audio and a photo of the people on the video. Our favorite video editing tools are iMovie, Nero, or Adobe Premier Pro.

The great thing about audio is that people can take it with them. If you're comfortable with video, and you know how to use it, we recommend both — record the video then extract the audio and use it everywhere audio podcasts are available. We use Libsyn to broadcast our podcast. You could use other services like Podbean, BuzzSprout, Soundcloud, or Anchor.fm. The audio is very powerful, because people can consume the content while they're doing other things. They can get to know you while they exercise, drive a car, work in the garden, walk the dog, or even while they cook. You become their friend, mentor, and leader directly through a podcast. That's the power of a podcast.

When you create your artwork for your podcast, you can hire a professional graphic designer or you can create the images yourself on Canva.com or Photoshop. There are free Photoshop classes on the Adobe website. We love using Canva.com for our artwork. You can create a YouTube thumbnail, social media posts, and artwork for Apple podcasts and more. Check it out at Canva.com.

https://www.canva.com/join/reflected-chefs-sparkle

How to Publish a book

At Elite Online Publishing, we publish on all bookstores online. We make sure to distribute the book in more than 40,000 libraries and retail locations. It's important to have your book available everywhere books are sold. If you are only on Amazon and your best friend only buys her books from Barnes and Noble on her Nook, then we have a problem.

You want to be very strategic about the Amazon book and Kindle categories. Categories on Amazon are very important. You want to make sure your book is submitted with the correct categories. We had an author come to us that paid a lot of money to publish his book. He had only three book categories listed for his eBook and paperback on Amazon. Shocked, we asked what happened. Usually Amazon gives you two categories when you submit your book. But we help our authors to add up to 10 categories on Amazon in each country.

I like to use this example: when remodeling a house or something even smaller — remodeling your bathroom. You could learn how to lay the tile, how to be a plumber, how to be an electrician, and everything else that goes along with it, *or* you could hire our company. We are the general contractor and we do *everything*. You just come in and brush your teeth afterwards. That's the difference. Think about where your time is best spent.

When it's time to publish a book, you want to publish with print on demand through Kindle Direct Publishing on Amazon and IngramSpark. That is what we do, we help our client self-publish the book. This way the client can order as many books as they need, *when* they need them. We do not recommend ordering 1,000 books or 5,000 books. Don't do it! Why do you need to have boxes and boxes of books in your garage? We had an author come to us who had 1,000 books in his basement — he invested more than $5,000 in print costs and he didn't know what to do with the books. Only order what you need. Put your money in your marketing and promotional budget. Use print on demand. If you're ordering any large number, say more than 50 or 100 books, then it's going to take a couple weeks to get them delivered, so keep that in mind. You're going to need a couple weeks lead time to get that many books.

What Format Will Your Book Be?

Next, it is time to decide your book formats: eBook, hardback, softcover, or audiobook. Why not have them all? A hardback or hardcover book is loved by collectors and die-hard readers or fans. Within the book industry it is known as *Trade Cloth*. The paperback is usually a flexible paper cover. It is usually a lower-priced edition of a hardcover book. An eBook is the most inexpensive price and can be read on an electronic device like a tablet, phone, laptop, or desktop computer. An audiobook is the most popular as we write this book. Digital audiobooks are the fastest growing type of format in publishing. In 2019, audiobook sales rose 16% in the USA. They generated $1.2 billion in revenue. In 2018, the revenue was $940 million. Audiobooks currently generate more money than eBook sales. An Edison Research national survey of American audiobook listeners ages 18 and up found that the average number of audiobooks listened to per year increased to 8.1 in 2020, up from 6.8 in 2019. The most popular audiobook genre continues to be mysteries/thrillers/suspense. Fifty-seven percent of frequent audiobook listeners are under the age of 45; this is up from 51% in 2019.

https://goodereader.com/blog/audiobooks/audiobook-trends-and-statistics-for-2020

Audiobooks are growing exponentially every year. There's the least amount of competition in audiobooks, because not that many people are doing them. You get more exposure for your book. As a bonus, Audible has something called a bounty. If someone buys your audiobook and signs up for Audible, then they send you a $75 bounty. The amount itself is not significant, if you're getting $30,000 for a client, but it's something extra. A bonus from your regular sales royalties.

Books published by Elite Online Publishing

For our clients, we start out with each author publishing an eBook and paperback. No matter what you know, you must have that Kindle eBook and why not do a printed paperback version as well.

If you are a public figure, and you have credibility in your field already, you would want all four formats. For example, we have an author who is a newscaster on major media networks. For her, she needs to offer an audiobook, hardback book, paperback, and eBook. She needs to look professional. That's the field she's playing. If you want to play big, you need to look like you are playing in the big leagues.

One of our clients is starting her own virtual marketing company and is just getting her feet wet. She does not have to publish on all four formats. For someone like her, we suggest she start with the eBook and paperback. That's how we differentiate ourselves from other publishers. We figure out where you are in your business, and if your goal is pursuing high-dollar clients. If so, you'd want to play in the big leagues and offer all formats of the book, including an audiobook. If you must sacrifice one of the formats, sacrifice either the paperback or the hardback and make sure you have an audiobook.

Bestseller Campaign

For each one of our authors we run our bestseller campaign. To do this, we set the price of the eBook to .99 cents for 24 to 48 hours. During that time, we use email marketing, social media marketing, word of mouth, and virtual book parties to propel your book to number one bestseller in multiple categories on Amazon. Sometimes we will promote the eBook in other countries like Australia, United Kingdom, and Canada to reach international bestseller.

Social Media image used for book release

So far, we are 100% in reaching our goal for each author to achieve bestseller status. This title gives the author a chance to stand out from their competition. Not only do they have a book, but they have a bestselling book. When they get introduced on stage or on a podcast interview, they are introduced as a #1 International Bestselling Author. Instant credibility. To some people this title isn't important. To those that feel this way, we explain to them that the bestseller status keeps your book on the top of the list on Amazon. Each time you hold a promotion and sell your eBook at .99 cents on Amazon, is a chance to push your book back up to the #1 spot in your category on Amazon. This gets more eyes on your book, which leads to more sales. Why not become a bestseller? You went to the effort to write your book. You deserve to sell a ton of books and become a bestseller.

6

HOW TO MAKE MONEY WITH A BOOK

— Jenn Foster

There are many ways to make money with a book, including a podcast. We're going to review several different methods and opportunities that a book will bring you.

In 2014, I wrote the book *Books to Bucks: The Top 20 Ways to Make Money with a Book*, with Everett O'Keefe. I was sitting in a marketing conference in San Diego. I was writing quickly in my notebook, taking notes with the panel speakers on stage. One of the speakers was Everett O'Keefe. I met Everett a few years back at the same conference. While he was talking, he said the words *Books to Bucks*. I wrote it in my notebook and talked to him later that night suggesting that we co-author a book together with that title! I was inspired by his words and knew it would make a great book. *Books to Bucks* goes into detail of the different ways you can make money with a book.

Everett O'Keefe on a panel in San Diego at the Marketing Conference

Ten Ways to Make Money from Your Book Today

#1 Web Page Giveaway

Give Your Book Away for Free — Not Your Service!

One way to draw attention and revenue is by creating a web page giveaway. This is where you will give your book away for free. It may seem contradictory at first, but a webpage giveaway is a great way to get your leads and to make money. It all starts with a landing page, which is a one-page website that asks for one's name and email in exchange for a free gift. It's called an opt-in and that free gift would be your book. It is an amazing way to leverage your book, because you're giving it away for free. Of course inside the book are ways your reader can work with you and become your client. There are several software options that can build the landing page for you, including: ClickFunnels, Infusionsoft, or MailChimp.

When creating a landing page you want to be sure to include a title for the page or a heading. Having a picture of you and or a video will help the reader know, like, and trust you. You will want to include the benefits of what they will read in your book. And last, but not least, your call to action. Create an opt-in form for them to enter their name and email. These five things are essential when creating a landing page. The following is an example of my *Books to Bucks* landing page. This page offers a free infographic after you buy the book. Be creative, you can use landing pages to give anything away, your book, a PDF, or infographic.

Example of the *Books to Bucks* landing page

#2 Pre-Frame a Meeting

One of our authors, Dr. Scott Hamblin, is a dental veneer specialist and cosmetic dentist, he wrote a book entitled: *The Naked Tooth*, which we thought was a fun title. His book talks about the fears of coming in and getting dental work done. He overcomes his clients' fears in the book. After they finish reading, they're ready to come in and sign. He easily can get the patient an appointment on his calendar and get their teeth fixed. I've seen it done with plastic surgeons too, but it's a great way to pre-frame the meeting for any industry. You have the unique opportunity to answer those questions and address concerns up front. They can read your book, and then they're ready to work with you.

As mentioned earlier, Steve also had an experience similar to this. A man bought his book. He didn't read it, but was ready to work with him just because he had the book. Steve had pre-framed his sales meeting. He closed the sale simply because the man owned a copy of his book.

3D mockup image of *Podcast Authorized* the book

#3 Foot in The Door: Getting Past the Gatekeeper

Number three — we love this one — the foot in the door strategy, also known as getting past the gatekeeper. Of course, Amazon is awesome, because we have Amazon Prime shipping. Did you know you can add a gift receipt or a gift note? This is a cool option. We use this foot in the door strategy all the time when we have a specific potential client we want to sign on. Once your book is published you can order the book from Amazon at the retail price, with a gift receipt, leave a little note, and even go a step further and offer a link to a video. This can be a short 30-second video on YouTube that is unlisted, which means that no one can see it, except the person who has the link. In the video or in the note, you can guide them to a specific page in your book that you know will help their business.

Personal note with a copy of her book from Cathy Fyock

Of course, if it's a CEO or corporation, it's going to need to go past that gatekeeper. The secretary is not going to open it. It's a package from Amazon. It's going straight to his desk; you're going to get your foot in the door and be right in front of your targeted potential client. We've even heard of a man who wrote a book specifically for two people. Not a *niche* — but actually just two individuals! They were billionaires who they wanted to have as clients. They mailed the book to them gift wrapped and included a note from Amazon. It worked! They closed a deal with one of the two as a client. It's really an awesome, very effective strategy!

#4 Meeting with a VIP or Celebrity

Remember earlier in the book, Melanie told the story of Mike Koenigs meeting with Richard Dreyfuss. Now, I don't think Richard would have talked to Mike if he only had a business card. Mike was able to get his book into Richard's hands. He wrote a note inside the book; something like this, *"Mr. Dreyfuss, I have an idea that will raise money and awareness for your organization."* He was able to sit right next to him on the flight home, which led to a working partnership. This strategy is totally awesome.

One of our clients, S.J. Flann, wrote a fiction book about technology and energy entitled: *Captain Glow*. She went to the Telluride Film Festival in Colorado and met Bill Gates. She sat in the front row, while Bill announced the release of *Inside Bill's Brain* on Netflix. Afterwards, they got to meet with Bill. She handed him a flyer for her book. Her book was for pre-order on Amazon and when the book came out, she mailed a copy of the paperback book directly to Bill and

Melinda Gates. Her book gives her the credibility to talk with and work with a celebrity or VIP, such as Bill Gates, which isn't easily obtained by other means.

Captain Glow by S.J. Flann. 3D mockup image

#5 Get Speaking Gigs

The fifth method is to get speaking gigs. We talk to so many authors who say they want to speak to multiple corporations and get booked to speak on stages, but if they don't have a book, they're not even going to be considered. One of our authors, Joshua Evans, wrote a book about being enthusiastic, *Enthusiastic You!* He's now books speaking engagements nationwide. In fact, he even was booked to speak on the Queen Mary. He is speaking to large corporations — and he gets paid to speak!

Of course, he includes his books in his speaking fee. He gets paid to fly there, gets paid to stay there, gets paid to speak and teach the content of his book. Everyone with whom he's speaking gets a copy of this book. It's awesome.

Joshua Evans: author, speaker, coach

#6 Trade Shows & Events

Ty Bennett is another person who does the same thing at trade shows and events where he speaks. His book, *The Power of Storytelling*, is sold or given to everyone with whom he speaks. Now, this is a great way to make money with your books. Of course, he has them in the back of the room to sell as well.

Jenn Foster and Ty Bennet at the National Speakers Association meeting in Salt Lake City, UT

I listened to Ty Bennett at a National Speakers Association. He attracts high-ticket customers with his book and gets paid a significant amount of money to speak. He brings his books with him in the room and offers them for sale. When we were there, he sold maybe 50 books in a crowd of about 100. Which wasn't a huge number of book sales, *but* every one of those individuals, if they own a corporation or run an event, are going to be asking him to come and speak for them. He's making considerable revenue just by having the book there as a means to get in touch with him.

#7 Call to Action

We touched on this a bit earlier, but we want to dive into it more now — you need to create a solid call to action. We want to make sure that all our authors include a call to action in their book. Having a *how-to* book is great, but if you don't include a call to action, no one is going to call you later to use your services. That is how you make money with the book, after all. You're not going to make significant money by selling actual physical books, you're going to make the *big* money by using them to promote your services. Your readers become your clients.

One of our authors, Lauren Golden, runs a company called: The Free Mama. She offers a digital training course where she teaches women how to quit their jobs, stay home, and be a virtual assistant at home. She helps moms find ways to stay home with their kids and earn money at the same time. In the book we published on her behalf, her call to action is to sign up for her training course. By joining her course, you learn how to be home, quit your job, and work as a virtual assistant. The first week her book came out, she became an international bestseller. During that first week, she told us that she had a client on one of her calls — they do a call every time they do the live training — and she said, "How did you find our training course?" Her client answered, "Oh, I bought your book from Amazon, so I joined!" In the *first* week of the book launch, she made money with her book! By making sure you have that right call to action, the possibilities are limitless!

Lauren Golden holding her book: *The Free Mama*

#8 Free Giveaways

That brings us to number eight — free giveaways. We've talked about this a lot. Giving your book away as a free eBook or PDF file. It's more than just giving the book away for free! Say your ideal client is a real estate person. Instead of just giving your book to a realtor, you actually could give 30 of your books to a realtor's office. Imagine what an impact that would have! If you had your book on the desk of every realtor in that office, it would be extremely impressive and quite awesome. You'd be getting a lot of clients from that!

You also can hold a contest on your Facebook page. You're giving away a physical copy of your book and you have a contest and they have to answer several questions or share the post and then you mail a copy to them.

Another effective way is by keeping a copy of your book with you always. In fact, we challenge our authors to do just that! Keep one in the trunk of your car, your office, your purse — everywhere! This gives you the opportunity to regularly have books available to give away. If you can give one book away each day, that's ideal! Of course, you want to do more if you can, but we challenge our authors to try and give at least one book away a day.

#9 Joint Ventures

Let's talk about joint ventures and how they can benefit you. Steve Gordon experienced this with his podcast. He got 15 people to be an affiliate for him and to share his book release. He garnered 5,000 leads — just like that — from those 15 affiliates. That quickly he garnered all those leads by creating the list of 15 affiliates who were going to help to promote him and increase his followers, therefore increase his leads.

Joint ventures are *very* beneficial. The first book I ever wrote was a joint venture. It was a compilation book with Dan Kennedy called *Stand Apart*. I wrote a chapter in that book, which included about 30 chapters total in the compilation book. That book changed my digital marketing business. Once I had the published book and it became a bestseller overnight, I was getting tons of phone calls. I even had one gentleman who called me from Idaho. In the voicemail, he said:

"It's three in the morning, and I can't sleep. I just read your chapter. I have a digital marketing agency here in Boise, and I realized I'm doing it all wrong. I need to hire you to service my clients. Do you have a white-label service? I want to use your company and implement all the strategies you're doing."

It was an empowering experience! There were a lot of people calling me because of that book — and I leveraged it! Dan Kennedy is the founder of Magnetic Marketing® and one of the most revered marketing advisors to entrepreneurs and business owners in the world. Dan has taught his Magnetic Marketing System to more than six million people around the world. The people who know him, associate *me* with him, *because* of this book. I took advantage of the opportunity to be in a compilation book with a marketing guru.

3D mockup image of *Stand Apart* book by Dan Kennedy and Jenn Foster

This is one of the things that our Mastermind group is doing right now. We're actually compiling an anthology book together. The title is *Authority*. We are going to be doing a marketing campaign with this book to reach the *Wall Street Journal* and *USA Today* bestseller lists.

#10 Media Attention and Press Releases

When you author a book, of course, you're going to want to distribute a press release. When our authors become bestsellers, we send out a press release and secure *tons* of media attention. They get asked to be a part of podcasts and even get booked for TV or radio interviews.

Now, if you don't know what you could write about, or you think, oh, what I know isn't really worth putting in a book. We think of our friend Sandi Masori's story — they called her the balloon lady. She knew how to tie balloons — making balloon animals like a clown. So, she wrote a book on how you can use balloons in your marketing and when you're doing trade shows to make your booth amazing. Her book is entitled: *The Ultimate Guide to Inflating Your Tradeshow Profits, How to Increase Branding, Recognition, Visibility, Customer Loyalty & Attract More Attention with Balloons!* She has written many more books as well. However, she wrote that book, and *because* of it, she was invited to be on multiple TV news spots. When she went on TV, she had her big balloons on her head. She even got the news anchors to wear balloons on their heads. The TV station *loved* it, because it brought so much attention to their station. She's been on the *Today Show* more than three times now. She was even on the *Home & Family Hallmark Channel* network. We don't believe they would have had her on the show if she didn't author a book. Books are that credible! They establish you as an expert — and her in case — the best balloon expert in the world! You *absolutely* need to have a book, if you want to get media attention.

Sandi Masori with the crew from the *Home & Family Show* on the Hallmark Channel

Bonus: Charge More Money

I'm going to give you one more idea. In my book: *Books to Bucks: The Top 20 Ways to Make Money with your Book (even if you haven't written it yet)*, we actually discuss 21 ways to make money. The bonus is when you have a book, you can charge more money for your services. Now you might think, *'Wait, it's still the same service and worth the same value and I can't charge more money.'* However, the truth is, when you write your book, your expertise jumps sky high, and you can charge more money for your services. When I started my digital marketing services, I didn't value my service as much as I should have. *Because* of that book, I raised my prices — and it's been amazing since then! You might think I would lose clients because of it, but the opposite is reality. I have sustained clients for more than seven years. They keep renewing their marketing services, because they realize the value I provide — I am the expert.

3D mockup image of *Books to Bucks* by Everett O'Keefe and Jenn Foster

Those are *my* top 10 ways to make money with *your* book. Of course, in my book we have 20 ways, but this list should give you some ideas you can implement right away to make money with your book.

7

PRODUCING A PODCAST AND PUBLISHING A BOOK

— Jenn Foster

Now we can brainstorm on how you can get your book, as well as get your podcast published and produced.

As we mentioned earlier, it's a good idea to send your book out to businesses. If you send out 20 books, that's 20 desks on which your book sits. Those individuals are going to know about you and your services, which is one of the keys to getting yourself out there!

For those of you who are selling into environments where you've got multiple decision-makers, part of your challenge is to create that elevator conversation, hallway conversation, or in current times, that Zoom

Video conference conversation. When talking to executives, let them know you've got a good book for them to read. Share the topic and mention how the book solves a challenge that they're experiencing. They will want to buy your book. When you can begin to engineer conversations like that, it becomes really powerful! There's nothing like it. You can't buy that kind of power.

Establishing Your Credibility with a Book

You may be wondering about compilation books or licensed books. We know a few of these books that are out there for realtors or other specific career titles. While we have seen some success with some compilation books, it's not recommended, because sometimes it is duplicate content. They change the cover of the book and the first chapter, but the rest of the book is the same. This doesn't look good on Amazon or Google. The books don't necessarily have the call to action and all the other aspects we've discussed. Given the choice between a compilation book and a single-author book, there's more credibility and more leverage in *you* being the author and having it be *your* book. If that's not a possibility for you, then go with a compilation book. However, a second choice would be to interview professionals in your field. At least then your name is still on the book cover. You now have content and not only that, but you can charge these individuals to be included in your book. Now *you're* the one making the compilation book. The third option would be to approach someone else and be a part of *their* book. Reaching out to a vendor, realtor, or other non-publisher to create a book would be the absolute last option. It's not specific to you. It's not specific to your brand. It doesn't share *your* story, and why you are the best realtor (or other professional) for your area.

Think of it this way — you want your name on it. You want to position yourself as *the* authority. We work with a lot of financial advisors. There are situations where you could basically buy the book and just put your name on it. Regulators in the financial industry have basically stated that you no longer can do that. It wouldn't be surprising if other industries, such as real estate, start putting those limitations in place as well.

We've also had a couple of places where we published books that have said they are no longer going to be publishing duplicate content books, only publishing quality books. If it's a duplicate content book, which is what these license books are, they're going to deny them. They're not allowing them anymore, because the quality isn't there. It's similar to Google, which doesn't like duplicate content. It needs originality.

Generally, those books are going to be printed for you, and you're going to have those copies, but you're not going to be published. That's an important difference here, especially when establishing credibility. People often get confused, thinking, *'Oh, I have an eBook!'* Well, your eBooks are on your website, but it's not anywhere else. Because of that, you're really *not* a published author and you're lacking that authority. Of course, you're a writer, but you're not considered an author until you are published. Being published is more than just where your book is available to purchase, it is the credibility that goes along with that. When you become a bestselling author, you have the credibility that enough people believed in your book. They bought your book, read it and now know that you are an expert in your field. We advise that you be careful if you get involved in one of those licensed books, because yes, it's putting your name on the cover and adding a few extra pages, but you're not on Amazon. You're not at Barnes and Noble. You're not at Walmart.com.

Establishing Your Credibility with a Podcast

Now that we've discussed ways in which a published book sets you apart and establishes credibility, let's explore how a podcast can do the same when executed properly.

Podcasts are becoming increasingly slick and well produced. If you're going to create a podcast that only exists to get a large listenership, then of course, the game has increased. For example, we mentioned Dan Sullivan earlier. His podcast, *Strategic Coach*, has 14 podcasts. Most are just Dan and somebody else talking on basically a telephone conference line. It's recorded and not edited in any way. There's no music at the beginning. In the end, it's about as low rent as you can get with a podcast. Ironically, those in particular are some of the ones ranked the highest, when looking at the top 100 business podcasts.

For this strategy to work though, the aspect you want to focus on is having a place to invite guests who can help you promote the book, and if you can do that, then it's worth doing — even if nobody listens. The production values don't matter, in most cases.

Depending on your demographic — who are you trying to reach — the approach may be different. Are you trying to reach the person looking for something that looks like you're on ABC News? If so, the audio quality is especially important. We're also finding that having an authentic voice is what differentiates the most popular podcasts from the rest. Those individuals aren't trying to be all fancy and formal. They're the ones who are authentic, casual, just being themselves. You feel like you're in the room having lunch with them or just hanging out having a conversation. The most successful ones are people who are true to themselves and authentic. Keep that in mind when you start producing your podcast!

One of our mentors is Ed Mylett. He hosts a podcast called: *The Ed Mylett Show*. All his content is professional and polished. He always has video bumpers or audio bumpers on everything. He has a professional edited preview at the beginning of his content. It's professionally edited and polished, but he is still real and authentic. With your podcast, it doesn't need to be professionally edited or have original music at the beginning. The current trend is to have all your content raw and real — to be vulnerable. Consider how many more views you get on a Facebook Live compared to a different video that you're doing that you're uploading onto Facebook.

TikTok is a great example of this. Many of the users are in their teens, but also adults. Even Dwayne "The Rock" Johnson is on TikTok. And there's more groups on TikTok, ranging from specific age groups, lifestyles, careers, and more, but they all have one thing in common — being real! Of course, they're using other videos, following trends, or using specific filters. On TikTok and even on Instagram, you'll notice some of the influencers are starting to not do the polished filtered photos. They are creating more raw, real, and vulnerable content. Just by being themselves, they're attracting more followers.

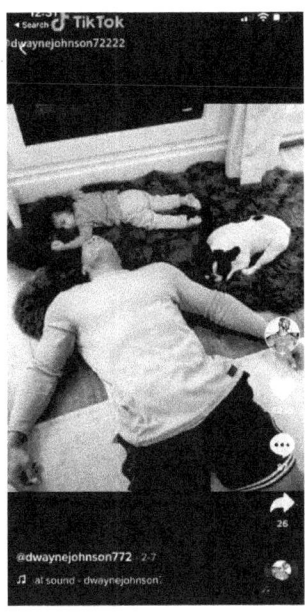
Dwayne Johnson "The Rock" on TikTok

The other big challenge with that, and this applies to books as well, is when you try to create something that is so polished, it actually becomes a barrier to you getting it done. It can lead to it being weak and you'll find that you keep editing it over and over. You need to have a little know-how on what you're doing. You need a good microphone and other recording equipment and software. Of course, getting it started is more important than any of those other technical concerns, because what you should do with both strategies that we're giving you is *commit to it!* Commit to one podcast a week. Or, maybe you only do two podcasts per month. Commit to it for one year. Who knows, you might be doing a podcast for the next decade. If you're smart, this gets you out of the day-to-day marketing.

Okay, now to get you out of the *'I need to get a million Instagram followers by the end of the week'* mindset. That's stressful. Steve Gordon will admit that he barely knows how to operate Instagram and is the guy that hits the heart button three weeks after something was posted, because he didn't open it in a timely manner. We don't want you to exist in that mindset. Whenever we're looking at how we're building our business, we want to focus on things that don't change. What we've laid out for you are strategies that actually haven't changed in decades. Sure, podcasting is a new technology, but we employed very similar techniques in our first business in the late 1990s and early 2000s. We would interview targeted potential clients, record the interview on a CD, and mail it. You could call it ghetto podcasting at its best, but it worked! We're talking about building relationships; the podcast is just a way to do that and is *very* effective. Books have been around *forever*. Commit yourself to building the foundation of your business on practices that aren't going to change and you're going to have a much easier experience.

Look at the 1950s and how broadcasting lifted the barrier. Radio has been around for decades. It lifted the barrier to everybody to be a radio host and have their own radio show, to have their own voice. It's the same thing with what Amazon did for publishing. Before, you had to go through a traditional publisher, but now it lifted that barrier and opened up to everyone else who has a story to tell. The way in which we deliver our products may change, but the products — the podcast or the book — stays the same!

Zoom screenshot of Melanie Johnson, Jenn Foster, and Juliet Clark on the Elite Expert Insider Podcast

You might be wondering how long your podcast episodes should be. A solid choice is 20 minutes, because that is about the average commute time in the U.S. However, the #1 podcast in existence is: *The Joe Rogan Experience* and it's about a three-hour show. Which makes the ideal time somewhere between 20 minutes and three hours.

The content matters more than the length. Rogan proved that if you have interesting content, people will listen. People will listen to a three-hour long podcast, if it's good quality. They will listen to it for 20 minutes on one car trip and then pause it and pick it up later in the afternoon. If it is quality, they will complete the whole thing.

Don't think of length as important right now. Don't let that be your focus. From a practical standpoint, implementing 20-30 minutes out of your day for your podcast and maybe allow a total of an hour for preparing the podcast and wrap up. At the start, you're building good rapport and establishing a relationship with the guests, but allow about 20-30 minutes of airtime for starting an episode.

When it comes to equipment, co-author Steve Gordon uses the Rode PodMic Dynamic Podcasting Microphone. We use the Blue Yeti microphone. Our editor recommended this one to me — but he didn't buy this until he was 18 months into his podcast. Don't let equipment be a stopping point for you!

Your laptop has a camera on it, use that! Your laptop also has a microphone, use that! Make sure you have good lighting when recording video. You can even put a table in front of a window where the window light is on your face. Then hit record. There you go! It's that simple! You can start a podcast with zero dollars for the production.

After all, if you're trying to run a business, just like with a book, ask for help. There's a time and a place for doing it yourself, but if you're already busy, find help! Whether you work with somebody like Steve or with us at Elite Online Publishing, on the book side of it. You build a team internally, because your job as the CEO, is to create that message, which will go in your book or podcast. It's to build the relationships that you're going to create through the podcast. That's your only role.

Now is the time. Get out there and create your podcast and your book.

Podcast + Book = Money

ABOUT THE AUTHORS

JENN FOSTER

Jenn Foster

Jenn is the co-owner of Elite Online Publishing and CEO of Biz Social Boom, a company dedicated to helping business owners of all sizes thrive in today's highly technical world of product and service promotion. Jenn owned and operated a successful local chain of retail stores, where she honed her online marketing skills. From local brick and mortar stores to online entities to large international corporations, Jenn's years of experience and expertise has now helped hundreds of businesses become front page news on all major search engines. She is dedicated to helping businesses use powerful new online and mobile marketing platforms to get visibility, traffic, leads, customers, and raving fans. Jenn is a 15 times international bestseller. As co-owner and CEO of Elite Online Publishing, she is passionate about helping busy entrepreneurs, business leaders, and professionals create, publish, and market their book, helping to build their business and brand. She encourages new authors to share their stories, knowledge, and expertise to help others. With her marketing and digital background, Jenn uses the best strategies for her clients' books to boost their sales and marketing platforms and make them #1 bestsellers.

A graduate of Utah State University, Jenn is an award-winning web designer, author, and sought-after speaker. She has been a featured panelist and speaker at events with experts like Loral Langemier, Lisa Sasevich, Mike Koenigs, Ed Rush, and more. Jenn has been named one of America's Premier Experts® and is highlighted in the Dan Kennedy Book: *Stand Apart*. Jenn Foster was recently named one of "Utah's Thought Leaders" in the book *Innovate Utah* by Global Village. Jenn is the co-host of *Elite Expert Insider* Podcast on iTunes and stitcher radio.

Coming from a family of successful entrepreneurs, her Grandfather started the Maverik Country Stores oil and gas station chain, which is still thriving today. Jenn grew up around successful businesses and understands from the ground up what it takes to create, run, and promote successful companies. Combining her education, knowledge, and life-long experience, today Jenn teaches people and businesses globally how they can get found in today's virtual world, how they can engage prospects on their terms and how to continue to connect and follow up with prospects to convert them to customers.

Jenn is a single mom who loves spending time with her three children, traveling, and experiencing the great outdoors.

Follow Jenn Foster:
AuthorJennFoster.com
Eliteonlinepublishing.com
Facebook.com/authorjennfoster
@jennfosterchic
Instagram.com/eliteonlinepublishing
YouTube.com/user/VideoFacebook101
YouTube.com/elilteonlinepublishing1

Elite Expert Insider: http://bit.ly/eliteexpertinsider

Book Jenn to Speak
Eliteonlinepublishing.com/speaking

COURSES:
Book Writing Fast Pass:
Bookwritingfastpass.com
Zero to Hero:
http://bit.ly/authorhero
Free Course:
5 Secrets to Marketing Your Book:
http://bit.ly/EliteFreeCourse

Journals: Elitejournals.com

PODCAST AUTHORIZED

MELANIE CHURELLA JOHNSON

Melanie Churella Johnson

Melanie launched, owned, and operated two independent TV stations in Houston and Dallas, Texas — Houston (Channel 51) and Dallas (Channel 55). Melanie started her career as a news anchor in Detroit at Channel 20 after she won the title of Miss Michigan and was first runner up to Miss America. Melanie has a background in media, marketing, public relations, and advertising. She has been in front of, as well as behind the camera. She was a news anchor, producer, writer, public relations, promotions, TV ad sales, programming negotiations, and financial strategist. She has conducted business with Warner Brothers, Disney, King World, and MGM Studios. In addition to creating and developing successful businesses, she has created award-winning advertising campaigns and is a 14 times #1 International bestselling author.

Melanie is the CEO and co-owner of Elite Online Publishing. They publish, market, and promote nonfiction books for business influencers and celebrities to create expert authority status for marketing impact and influence. She is passionate about sharing stories that educate, motivate, and inspire. She is honored to work one-on-one with authors to create the best strategies for their book creation, marketing, and social media.

Melanie was honored to be a TEDx speaker in Sugarland, Texas in 2016, where she spoke on the importance of leaving a legacy. She is the co-host of the *Elite Expert Insider* podcast on iTunes and Stitcher Radio and has a YouTube channel.

She got her feet wet in the luxury building and design industry when she was the general contractor and developer for her personal 25,000-square-foot home known as *The Houston Mansion* and her 13,000-square-foot summer home in Petoskey, Michigan, *The Walloon Lake House*. During the economic downturn, Melanie turned both properties into successful luxury vacation and event rental properties and continues to invest and develop real estate.

She is the CEO of Charity Auction Consignments. Melanie graciously donates her villa in the Dominican Republic, along with her other properties to help raise money for children's issues, health, education, and animals. She works with numerous charities including Texas Children's Hospital, Citizens for animal protection, Fanatical Change

Foundation, Just Like My Child, and a variety of private schools.

Melanie graduated from Michigan State University with a degree in communications and was the first female to receive a varsity letter in a boy's sport in the state of Michigan. Originally from Michigan, she resides in Houston, Texas. She is enjoying raising her two sons, who keep her motivated and young. She loves the beach, traveling, and spending time with her family.

Follow Melanie:
AuthorMelanieJohnson.com
Facebook.com/melanie.c.johnson.58
Instagram.com/melaniecjohnson
YouTube.com/elilteonlinepublishing1

Elite Expert Insider: http://bit.ly/eliteexpertinsider

Book Melanie to Speak
Eliteonlinepublishing.com/speaking

COURSES:
Book Writing Fast Pass:
Bookwritingfastpass.com
Zero to Hero:
http://bit.ly/authorhero
Free Course: 5 Secrets to Marketing Your Book:
http://bit.ly/EliteFreeCourse

Journals: Elitejournals.com

STEVE GORDON

Steve Gordon

Steve Gordon is the author of five books, including the Amazon Business #1 bestseller Unstoppable Referrals: 10x Referrals, Half the Effort, and Podcast Prospecting: How to Land High-Ticket Clients with a Podcast. He's the host of The Unstoppable CEO™ podcast and has appeared on more than 100 podcasts. His firm helps digital agencies, consultants, and expertise-based businesses systematically attract more clients.

At age 28, Steve Gordon became the CEO of an engineering/consulting firm. It was baptism by fire... Steve knew nothing about marketing or selling services. His firm got all its business by word of mouth, and they enjoyed a healthy, growing business. However, they never knew from where the next client was coming, or when the client would arrive. Steve spent countless nights staring at the ceiling at 2 a.m., worried about when the next client might come. So, he began studying sales and marketing.

Twelve years later, after growing that firm's revenue 10-times, Steve started his second business, consulting with other expertise-based businesses to design sales, marketing, and referral systems for high-ticket/high-trust products and services. Today, he continues sharing his expertise with clients across the world, opening their eyes to their unique growth opportunities and helping them build the right systems to attract their ideal clients.

Follow Steve at:
steve@unstoppableceo.net

Download his latest book, free, at
Unstoppableceo.net/exponentialnetwork

Acknowledgments

Thank you to our families for your support in all of our endeavors. Thank you to our clients who are amazing, we couldn't do what we do without you. Thank you to our strategic partners and our winning relationships.

Thank you for reading! Please add a short review on Amazon and let us know your thoughts!

BONUS
From Jenn Foster and Melanie Johnson:
Easily write your book using our **Mindset Tool Kit.**

Visit EliteOnlinePublishing.com/bonus

Mindset Toolkit

From Steve Gordon:

Download my latest book *free* at

UnstoppableCEO.net/exponentialnetwork

The Exponential Network Strategy the book

www.ingramcontent.com/pod-product-compliance
Lightning Source LLC
Chambersburg PA
CBHW071212070526
44584CB00019B/3004